AF893924

3 DANCES FOR SOLO TIMPANI

to Neil Grover

By Robert M. McCormick

1. **Waltz**
2. **Mystical Dance**
3. **Tango**

Alfred Music
P.O. Box 10003
Van Nuys, CA 91410-0003
alfred.com

ISBN-10: 0-7579-1823-9
ISBN-13: 978-0-7579-1823-0

Timpani Key

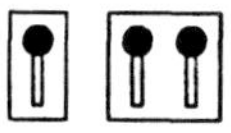 Staccato Timpani Mallets

 Wood End of Mallets

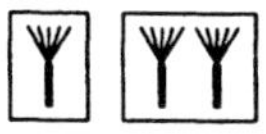 Wire Brushes

 Medium Felt Timpani Mallet

 Play on struts of timpani.
Vary timbre by striking different areas of struts and with different parts of the beater.

 Play in center of head.

 Cover low G timpani with cardboard head protector and play in center.

 Cover low G timpani with cardboard head protector and play at edge.

Performance Suggestions

Tempi should be flexible (not too metric) to enhance the stylistic qualities of the dances.

The chosen pitches may be written below the best sound quality range of the some timpani. If a warm sound can not be produced, it is acceptable to transpose the pitches up or substitute 26 and 23" drums with 29 and 26" drums.

Stick choices will vary depending on the size and ambience of the performance hall.

Melodic lines should be emphasized over accompaniment lines.

3 Dances for Solo Timpani

to Neil Grover

Rubato

1. Waltz

Robert M. McCormick

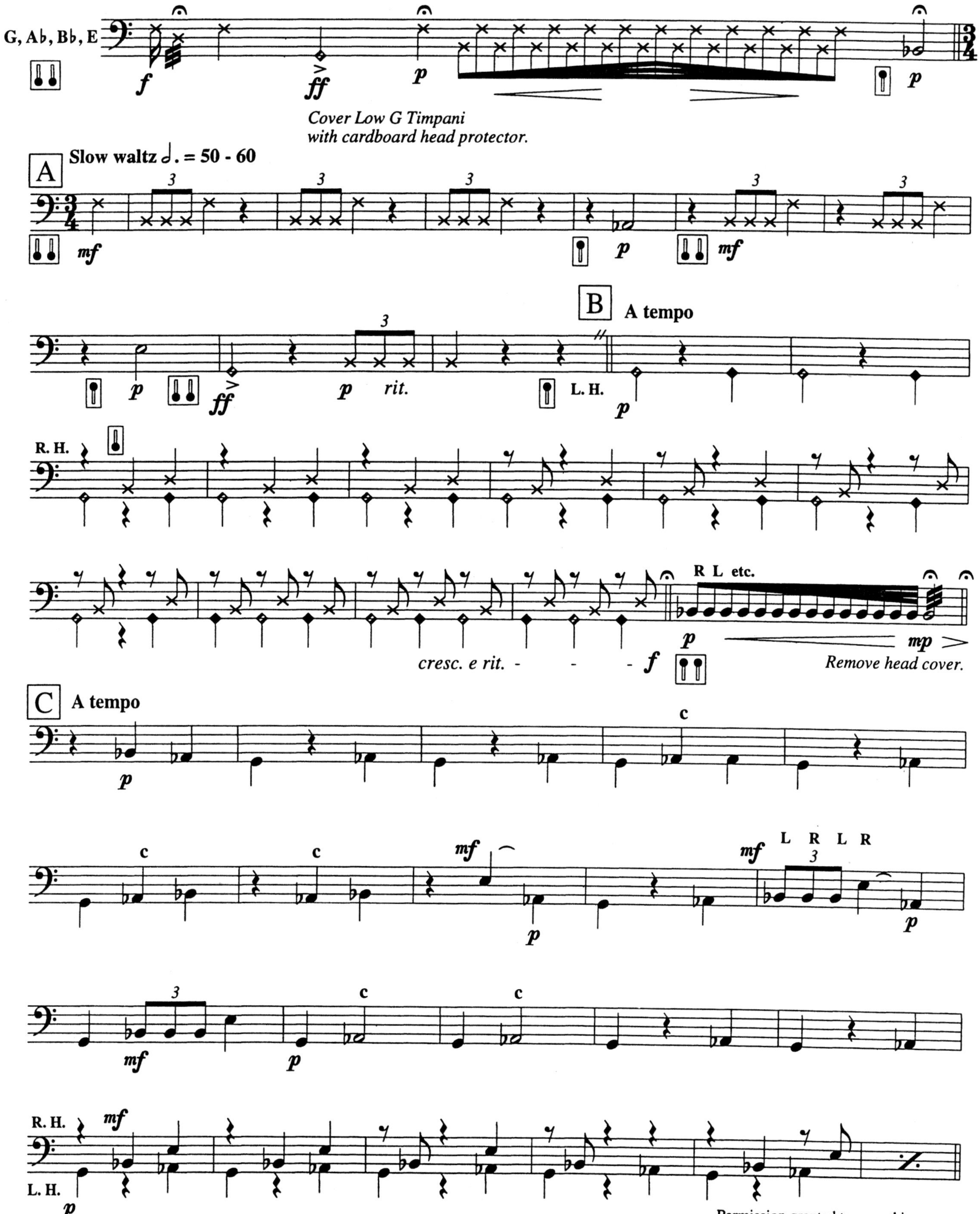

D
Rubato
p
cresc.
A tempo
f
p
c
mf
E
mp
Rubato
F
A tempo
agitato
G
ff

H
accel.
I
Rubato
cresc.
J
A tempo
A tempo
rit.
gliss.

2. Mystical Dance

C
R. H.
mf
L. H.
c
p
c
c
c
sim. to Letter D
gliss.
gliss.
D
Cadenza - Freely
f
p
accel. e cresc.
f
rit. e dim.
p
E
Slow and dramatic
ff
16
16

F
Allegro ♩ = 140
G, B♭, C, D♭
mp
rit. morendo
Andante rubato
p
L. H. Rapid
Swish
Pickup timpani mallet while swishing with left hand.

3. Tango

C
♪ = 260
f
gliss.
c c
ff
p
dim. e rit.
D
♩ = 90
mp
cantabile

E
♩ = 130
cantabile
rit.
a tempo
dim. e rit.
a tempo
a tempo
c to edge
c to edge
rit.
a tempo

Program Notes

Three Dances for Solo Timpani was written in 1998 and dedicated to percussionist Neil Grover. The Dances can be performed as individual solo works or together as a suite. Melodic intervals and timbre contrasts provide color for each dance. Subtle ambiguity in rhythm, pulse, and pacing create a challenge for the performer and listener. The composer was influenced by several different styles and periods of music in the writing of Three Dances.

Biography

Robert M. McCormick is currently Professor of Music at the University of South Florida. He is a former member of the Harry Partch Ensemble and served as Principal Percussionist of the Florida Orchestra for twenty years.

Robert has a number of recording credits and had authored articles, solos and two texts: Percussion for Musicians (pub. Warner Bros.); and 32 Duets for Percussion (G. Schirmer). Robert also tours with the McCormick Duo, a flute/percussion ensemble, formed with his wife, Kim.